THE
STOUT
BOOK

BRENDAN O'BRIEN

ANNA LIVIA

First Published in 1990 by
Anna Livia Press Ltd.
21 Cross Avenue
Dun Laoghaire
County Dublin

Designed by John Power
Typeset by The Works
Printed in Ireland by Colour Books Ltd.

ISBN 1 871311 09 8

CONTENTS

ACKNOWLEDGEMENTS

My thanks are due to:
Syd Bluett, for starting it all one fateful afternoon in Peter's Pub;
Aongus Collins for his constant encouragement and editorial expertise;
John Doyle and Fergus Corcoran for seeing it through;
Tom Mathews for permission to reproduce his cartoons;
Vince Giltenan, Peter Hanan, Colin Johns, Tommy Hosford and
Dan O'Neill at Murphy's for their time and courtesy;
Peter Walsh at Guinness for his assistance and Joe Kennedy and John Molloy
for being such enthusiastic research assistants.
Jim D'Arcy, for his brewing expertise.
For information regarding their particular brews, I am grateful to:
Stephen Simpson-Wells (Raisdale), Carol Scott (Guinness),
Barry Newman (Shakespeare), Philip Douglas (Strzelcki),
Jim Reeves (Sovereign), Brenda Kruger (Castlemaine Perkins),
A. Ross (Samuel Smith), M.H. Rodrigo (Ceylon), A.D. Jacob (Tasmanian),
Rob Strong (The Loaded Dog), Dr. Simon Brooke-Taylor (Eagle Hawk Hill),
Howard Cearns (Matilda Bay), Stuart McLean Ramsay (Bridgeport),
Steve Harrison (Sierra Nevada), Michael Lovett (Mendocino),
Donald McCorkindale (Grants), E.H. Kristiansen (Wiibroe),
Robert Mayne P.R. (Coopers), Baron Heinrick Von Echte (Nussdorf),
Jorgen Orbech (Carlsberg), R.W. Luscombe (Watney Truman),
Jan Goodchild (Cornish),

I have relied for direction on the work of Michael Jackson, whose comprehensive
'New World Guide to Beer' is highly recommended to those who may wish to
pursue further the subject of beer worldwide.

INTRODUCTION

Should but the muse descending drop
A slice of bread and mutton chop
Or kindly when his credit's out
Surprise him with a pint of stout

Jonathan Swift

*Every day,
7,000,000 glasses
of Guinness are
drunk in over
130 countries.*

MR. HARWOOD'S BREW

The darkness we now know as stout first came to light - possibly by accident - in 1722, three years before Arthur Guinness was born. For centuries up to this the word 'stout' had been used to describe strong beers: it meant 'stout' as in 'stout ale'. This strength may have been in terms of taste or alcohol, or both. Jonathan Swift referred to a 'pint of stout' in a poem written in 1720, but that pint probably bore little resemblence to what we understand by the phrase today.

The dark brew we call stout is distantly related to an early eighteenth century drink called 'Entire'. If you called for this, you would be given a cocktail of three different ales. A London brewer, Ralph Harwood, produced Entire as a single brew in 1722. But, whether by accident or design, Mr. Harwood included in his mash a portion of malt which had been roasted beyond the normal limits. This gave the beer an unusual dark hue. The result, according to legend, was so popular with the city's market porters that it became synonymous with them. Thus was Stout Porter born.

The brew rapidly became Britain's most popular alcoholic beverage and breweries were soon competing to supply it. The term 'stout porter' became common in the 1920s. An 'extra stout porter'was a stronger, more full bodied version. Gradually the word 'stout' made the transition from adjective to noun, until eventually porter was superseded by its cousin which we now know as stout. It faded from British bars around 50 years ago, but survived in Ireland until 1973. Today the main hope for the survival of porter lies in small, modern breweries: many of these independents still produce it.

Above top: that all too familiar harp that comes on a brown envelope and bottom: the happier version used by Guinness.

éıre

3p

**ARTHUR
GUINNESS**

**Above: the
Republic of Ireland
honours Arthur
Guinness.**

THE GUINNESS DYNASTY

Arthur Guinness was in his seventies when the decision was made to devote his brewery exclusively to the porter which would immortalise his name. From what we know of the original Arthur, there emerges a picture of an ambitious, hard-talking, aggressive and fiercely determined chief executive... a sort of J.R. Brewing. For Dallas, read Dublin. For oil, read stout. Indeed, Arthur was probably just as interested in banking as in brewing.

Spirits like whiskey, gin and poteen were more popular and more reliable than beer in the Ireland of his time.

Arthur's son, also named Arthur, improved the quality of the family's 'Extra Superior Porter' and increased production. And *his* son, Benjamin, turned the largest brewery in Ireland into the largest brewery in the world. And so Benjamin begat Edward and Edward begat Rupert and Rupert begat Arthur again who begat Benjamin again. And so it came to pass that the Lord Iveagh said: "Let there be dark".

And there was Dark. Millions and millions of gallons of it, as Guinness continued its domination of the world stout market in the nineteenth century, exporting to Australia, Africa and Asia.

Guinness is now among the top 20 drink companies in the world. It operates breweries in countries as far apart as Ireland, Nigeria, Ghana, Cameroon, Malaysia and Sierra Leone. Increasingly, also, Guinness is being brewed under licence by fellow giants such as Carlton United (Australia) and Labatt's (Canada). All in all, Guinness is brewed in 30 countries worldwide.

The facade of Mountjoy Brewery, from Russell St.

IN THE
BEGINNING
WAS
THE WORT

*When I die, I want to decompose in a barrel of porter and have it
served in all the pubs of Dublin.*

J.P.Donleavy

A brewhouse circa 1750.

A s every home brewer knows, alcohol is formed by the chemical interaction of sugar and yeast. Theoretically, ordinary, commercial sugar could be used. In brewing, however, the

ONE PINT OF STOUT CONTAINS:	
200	KILOCALORIES
0.18 grms.	PROTEIN
17.4 grms.	ALCOHOL
25.2 grms.	SUGARS
138 milligrams	SODIUM (SALT)
270 milligrams	POTASSIUM
48 milligrams	CALCIUM
0.30 milligrams	IRON
0.48 milligrams	COPPER
0.24 milligrams	RIBOFLAVIN (B2)
2.58 milligrams	NIACIN (B3)
0.06 milligrams	PYRIDOXINE (B6)
0.06 milligrams	PANTOTHENIC ACID
0.66 micrograms	VITAMIN B12
26.4 micrograms	FOLIC ACID
3.0 micrograms	BIOTIN

sugars contained in barley are preferable to those derived from cane or beet.

The basic constituent of stout is barley, which consists mainly of starch. This starch is not soluble in water, and is not fermentable. So during the malting process, it's converted to sugar which is fermentable.

This transformation is effected by chemical middlemen called enzymes which are produced when barley germinates. This happens during malting. If soaked in water at the correct temperature and given enough oxygen, barley will germinate. At the maltings, it gets a warm bath for two days at 15° - 20°C. Then it is spread out on a flat surface and allowed to germinate: during this time the barley is constantly turned to allow heat and air circulate. The barley is heated for another day or so at 85° - 100°C to stop further germination.

The barley, which has become malt, is then roasted. The more it is roasted, the less fermentable the malt is. Therefore, most of it is just lightly roasted to give a **pale malt:** this constitutes about three quarters of the malt used. The very highly roasted **dark malt**, on the other hand, is 500 times darker and adds its distinctive colour as well as flavour to the pint. In between these

An early Guinness label.

extremes there are other levels of roasting, and other malts: amber malt, brown malt, crystal or caramel malt.

Barley may also be roasted like coffee without any previous germination/malting. Such **roasted barley** is added, particularly in dry stouts, to contribute flavour and colour.

At the breweries the various malts are mixed in the required proportions and then ground in a mill to produce **grist**. The grist is poured into a large vat and warm water is added to produce a **mash**. This souplike mixture is allowed to infuse, like tea, for about two hours at 60°C. This is when the starch is transformed by the action of enzymes into sugar. The resulting sugary liquid, called **wort**, is drained off, leaving behind a spent grain residue which is sold as animal feed.

It is at this stage that hops are added, and boiled with the wort for one or two hours.

Hop plants grow up to 20 feet high, and have to be supported by poles and wire. They're harvested for their flower which is green, cone-shaped and an inch long. The flowers can be compressed into pellets, reduced to a liquid extract or turned into powder form. Traditionally, brewers used dried hops, but now prefer less bulky hop pellets.

When boiled for an hour or two, the hops release oils and **resins** which provide a characteristic **bitterness** and **aroma.** They also act as a preservative, by preventing the growth of bacteria. Plant acids called Tannins are also produced which help to clear the stout.

For the brewer, the most

At Jame's Gate, Guinness employ centrifugal force as a method of yeast extraction.

Above: Castle Maine Brewery in its early days.

interesting content of the hop is the resin **humulon.** (also known as Alpha Acid). This determines the level of bitterness, which may be measured according to a scale devised by the European Brewery Convention. Among Irish Dry Stouts, for example, Guinness rates 45-48 European Units of Bitterness, Beamish 40 and Murphy 36 to 38.

To a large extent, the art of the brewer lies in balancing the flavour of the malt against the bitterness of the hops. Indeed, this bitterness might also be set off against other flavours in the brew. One American brewer, Bert Grant of Yakima, prides himself on using five times more hops than any commercial beer in his Imperial Stout.

Because hop varieties differ in their oil and resin content, some are valued for their bitterness while others are more likely to be

included at a later stage in order to impart aroma. The hops used in the brewing of

The brewer may choose to add to the stout some sweet wort which will interact with the residual yeast when bottled. This process is referred to as Krausening.

STOUT TRIVIA

SCRAECH

European Units of Bitterness are

(a) An obscure Dutch rock group

(b) The basis on which the Treaty of Versailles was agreed

(c) A method of measuring bitterness in beer

Answer: (c) is correct. It won't say so on the bottle, but chances are that your favourite stout contains 40 EUBs ■

stout are likely to be more bitter than those used in other beers such as lager.

After they've been boiled, the spent hops are removed from the wort. This is cooled to room temperature and transferred to a fermentation vessel.

There, yeast is added and fermentation begins. Yeast is a fungus- like plant. Highly sensitive to temperature, it is very much a living organism with a phenomenal capacity for reproduction, doubling every two hours under the right conditions. Brewer's yeast, known to the botanists as Saccharomyces Cerevisiae is distinct from traditional baker's yeast. For generations, Guinness has been cultivating a strain called Sacch-aromyces Cereosial.

Yeast plays a vital part in the brewing process by feeding on sugars to produce alcohol and carbon

BREW-IT-YOUR-SELF

There are a number of good reasons for brewing your own stout. It's a better introduction to the brewing process than a dozen diagrams or brewery visits. And then there's the satisfaction of producing your own distinctive product. After that, the joy of snatching loot from the revenue is only a minor consideration. But, be warned - it won't necessarily be a doddle.

The centuries of expertise which have gone in to the production of that ubiquitous bottle of Guinness will not be equalled overnight in your humble kitchen. And unless you're prepared to stick with it, your initial outlays may not pay off in long-term profits.

You will need to buy basic equipment which you won't find in the average kitchen - a large saucepan or boiler capable of holding a few gallons of liquid, a plastic fermentation bin or two, hydrometer, thermometer, funnels, cups, bottle, brush, etc... And that's before you buy the ingredients...

At the most basic level you can buy a kit containing hopped malt extract and yeast. While this may be adequate if you simply want to produce a drinkable lager, you are less likely to be satisfied with the resulting stout and will probably revert to the commercial variety. It is fair to say that you are unlikely to continue producing home-brewed stout unless you strive for excellence in taste. And this will only result from the use of top-quality ingredients such as fresh hops, various types of malt and an excellent yeast. Can your supplier offer a range of pale malt, roasted malt, crystal malt, black malt, as well as flaked barley and roast barley? Are you prepared for the mess and hassle involved? If you answer "yes" to these questions, you could be well on your way to brewing your own ■

Opposite Page:

Picking hops

**Above: Drinking
companions from
Harry Kernoff
R.H.A.**

*Brewers refer to
the water used in
the manufacture
of stout as 'liquor'*

dioxide, the gas without which any pint would be dead and flat. It also adds a distinctive flavour.

During fermentation, yeast rises to the top of the liquid to form a cauliflower head which may be as deep as three feet. (Lager production, on the other hand, uses a bottom-fermenting strain). After several days, during which the yeast and sugar have been interacting vigorously, the liquid is siphoned off, leaving a yeast sediment behind, and allowed to mature in large storage vats for periods ranging from 10 days to six months.

The stout is still 'alive' in the sense that any remaining yeast will continue to feed off residual sugars and produce natural carbonation (carbon dioxide). If this is allowed to continue, the consumer will enjoy naturally conditioned stout. (Naturally conditioned stout such as bottled Guinness contains a sedimentary residue of yeast which, if collected carefully, can be used to good effect in home brewing).

However, the brewer may use filtration to clear the beer of remaining yeast, or pasteurise it to extend its shelf life.

Light beers such as lagers are almost universally filtered to give a cosmetically attractive finish. But stout can hide unsightly cloudiness in its dark colour. Most important, however, filtration removes vital taste elements. And the heating involved in the pasteurisation process results in dead yeast with the end of any further natural carbonation.

And finally, a vital ingredient which might be taken for granted... water!

Below: one quarter of a million wooden barrels once stood in the cooperage yard of St. James Gate.

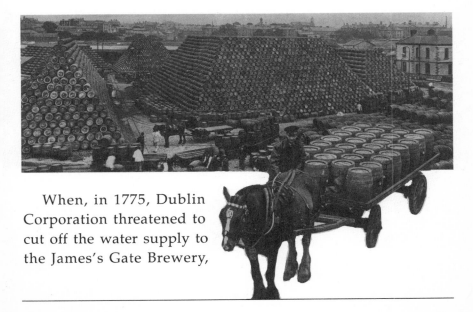

When, in 1775, Dublin Corporation threatened to cut off the water supply to the James's Gate Brewery,

Arthur Guinness 'gave for answer that the water was his and he would defend it by force of arms', daring them 'to try how far their strength would prevail'. When workmen arrived to fill in his water channel he seized a pick-axe from one of them, 'declaring with very much improper language that they should not proceed'... and that 'if they filled it up from end to end,

PUTTING THE EEs INTO BEER

Unless otherwise stated, beers are likely to contain small quantities of chemical additives as by-products of the brewing process. If most drinkers are blissfully unaware of this, it's because the legal requirements on the labelling of food ingredients do not apply to alcoholic drinks.

Additives widely used in brewing stout include:

Sulphur Dioxide (E220)
Phosphoric Acid (E338)
Sodium Alginate (E401)
Ammonia Caramel (E150(c))
Bentonite (E558)
Calcium Sulphate (E516)
Propylene Glycol Alginate (E405)

While the major danger is that such chemicals could set off an allergic reaction, an unhappy mixture could also give drinkers hangover symptoms ■

he would immediately re-open it'. Faced with such determined opposition, the Corporation backed off, but it would be another 10 years before the dispute would finally be resolved.

However, by 1868, the water supply which Arthur Guinness had gone to such lengths to preserve was no longer adequate

A billion Australian dollars was the sum paid by the legendary financier Alan Bond for Toohey's Brewery.

for what was by then the largest brewery in the world. Arrangements were made to have water piped from the Grand Canal in St. James's Well, in Co. Kildare. This source was adequate for 120 years. Today, if you ask for a glass of tap water in a Dublin pub,

*The German
purity Law,
which dates back
to 1516,
stipulates that
only water, malt,
hops and yeast
may be used in
the brewing of
beer.*

you will be given a clear liquid from the source now used by Guinness - the Dublin City Water Supply.

Most large breweries are content to draw from the local water supply, which may be treated to their own specification. The stout brewer generally prefers his water to be closer to the soft end of the scale, but may sometimes add gypsum to increase hardness. This concept of 'soft' and 'hard' water normally presents itself to the average householder merely as a minor irritation at the bathroom or kitchen sink.

If you have very little difficulty working up a lather from a bar of soap in your bathroom, it is reasonable to assume that the water pouring through your taps has been filtered predominantly through sandstone, is high on salts and may be described as 'soft'. If, on the other hand, you have a problem with 'fur' in your electric kettle, your tap water has probably travelled through limestone, contains traces of chalk and is described as 'hard'.

But then, as every home-brewer knows, only a fraction of the water used in brewing finds its way into the final product. The rest is needed for the endless washing and sterilising.

THE
GOOD
PINT

The barman fills the tumbler slowly, taking black stuff from several taps, and builds up a head worthy of the body.

John D. Sheridan

S tout is synonymous with Ireland. Nowhere is stout as popular or as intrinsically part of everyday life. Where else does a barman automatically interpret a call for 'a pint' as a request for the national drink? With their stained glass, polished wood, marble shining counters brass fixtures and subdued lighting, some of the older and more traditional pubs of Dublin at times take on the aspect of religious shrines, where drinking other than the ruby nectar is tantamount to heresy.

The criterion by which a pub is judged is likely to be whether or not it sells a good pint. The precise qualities and causes of a good pint have enlivened many a pub conversation. Does the barman clean the draught lines regularly? Are the glasses properly washed? Are the kegs stored in the basement or in a cold-room? Is there a high turnover? At the other extreme, many stomach upsets have been attributed to that ultimate nightmare, the bad bottle.

Most controversy surrounds the ritual pulling of the pint. Prior to the use of modern draught dispensing equipment, this did involve a degree of skill. However, with properly maintained equipment and a little patience, today's pint-pulling is child's play. Indeed, Irish exporters have made special efforts to convince barmen used to pulling instant lagers that stout requires a little more time and patience.

In Irish pubs, the poor quality of foreign stout is a topic on which you will hear very little argument. It is a subject for which the most derisive epithets are

In a famous legal judgement, the Guinness head was declared to be part of the drink.

Health Peace & Prosperity, an eigtheenth century view of the virtues of Porter.

reserved. And with some justification, for only in Ireland is draught Guinness not pasteurised, a process which purists believe adversely effects the taste. While most large commercial brewers pasteurise their products in order to improve their shelf-life, the huge turnover which Guinness enjoys in Ireland allows it to forego this form of sterilisation.

Setting aside pishogues and fallacies, let's look at some of the objective criteria for assessing a good pint.

Alcoholic strength does not automatically make for drinkability. It has, however, been of interest to bureaucrats as well as brewers, resulting in a variety of systems of measurement.

Original gravity is a measurement of predicted alcoholic content, based on the density of the pre-fermentation ingredients compared with water. While standard stouts such as Guinness, Mackeson and Samuel Smith will hover around 1040°, the more potent Russian Imperial Stouts and Foreign Extra Guinness are more likely to top 1070°.

Of more value to the consumer is a system of measurement based on **Alcohol by Volume** (ABV). This is a measurement of alcohol content after fermentation, expressed as a percentage. Under this system, your standard stout will range from 4% to 5%, while strong stouts such as the Australian Barley Stout reach as high as 7.9%.

European Community legislation now

The strongest beer in the world measured by ABV is "Roger and Out"(16.9 ABV; 1125 OG) brewed by the Frog and Parrot, Sheffield, England.

requires that ABV be displayed on all packaging.

And to confuse the matter further, alcoholic content is also measured in terms of Alcohol By Weight.

The Head consists of tiny bubbles of gas which have become coated in proteins and dextrins as they rose to the top of the drink. The head produced on pouring draught stout is of a denser, more viscous quality than that of bottled stout. This is because, unlike the bottling process, modern draught dispensers pump nitrogen gas as well as carbon dioxide into the drink. As nitrogen is less soluble than carbon dioxide, and has a smaller bubble size, the head formed is denser and lasts longer.

However, the formation and retention of the head are also determined by the quality of the brewing process and the ingredients. If sugar is used as a cheap substitute for malt, for example, the head will suffer. It is also important that economies are not made at the expense of the quality and quantity of the hops. Good quality hops, containing high levels of the resin, humolon are vital. If the mashing stage is not properly monitored, the necessary proteins and

**Woodcut of a
Dublin Character
by Harry Kernoff,
R.H.A.**

POURING DRAUGHT STOUT

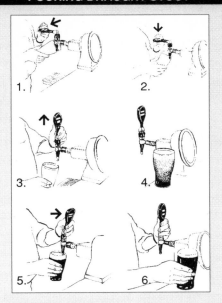

The strongest beer in the world measured by Original Gravity is Doomesday Ale (15.86 ABV; 1143 OG), brewed by the Cornish Brewery Company Ltd., Redruth, Cornwall.

(1) Holding a clean glass at an angle to the tap, the barman pulls the handle towards himself to a horizontal position.

(2) The stout flows down the glass, filling it to within half an inch of the rim.

(3) The tap is then shut off by releasing the handle to vertical.

(4) The stout is allowed to settle on the counter for approximately one minute.

(5) As a final touch, the barman tops off the head using the 'creamer', by pushing the handle slightly in the opposite direction, towards the customer.

(6) The head should be 'proud' of the rim, without overflowing. The time elapsing between ordering and first sip should not exceed 3 to 4 minutes.

Below: Cartoon by Tom Mathews.

dextrins will not materialise. Equally, proper conditioning is needed to produce the all-important carbon dioxide.

The extent to which the sugars have been fermented is another factor. If a fraction of the original gravity remains, the head will benefit, while fermenting all sugars down to zero gravity will have the opposite effect.

It is also possible to stimulate the head chemically. Propylene glycol alginate (E405) is widely used as a head-retaining agent in the brewing of beers, including stouts.

Recent attempts to achieve a 'draught' head from canned or bottled stout involve adding nitrogen to the drink. The gas is

subsequently released by agitation.

Finally, the colour of the head may depend to some extent on the ingredients used. You get a whiter head from barley which has only been roasted and not malted.

TEMPERATURE

Stout, with its roots in colder climes, has traditionally been a winter brew. Comments such as 'typically consumed in the dark winter months', 'a seasonal beer brewed only in winter' and 'often favoured in the colder months' are regularly used by stout-brewers world-wide. It is also a drink more suited to 'quiet, reflective sipping', than to guzzling by the gallon to slake dry-throated thirsts.

This doesn't make it any easier for the marketing manager of a commercial stout brewery whose job it is to move as much of the stuff as possible all-year round. Murphys, who recommend a serving temperature of 8°C, admit that as the weather gets warmer, sales of stout drop. Guinness is served cooler in summer than in winter. But who decides what 'cooler' means? Try defrosting your tastebuds after a typical glass of Guinness in Queensland,

Some of the older Murphy brewery workers like to drink their stout 'porter style' - left on a gas heater for a few minutes before consumption.

Australia served at zero degrees Centigrade!

It is difficult to avoid the conclusion that, in recent years, serving temperature has become a pawn in the rear-guard action being fought by stout producers against the onslaught of lagers. In an early 1958 television commercial, a barman recommended that Guinness be kept at room temperature in Summer and cool in Winter.

Cellar temperature (13°C/55°F) is the ideal serving temperature of stout. The American brewers Grants recommend that their Imperial Stout be served at 55°F. Mendocino Brewing Co. which produces Black Hawk Stout, says that it is 'best served at the traditional temperature of 50°- 60°, since ice-cold temperatures would mask the fine flavour'. The lower the serving temperatures of our stout, the less likely we are to experience the hundreds of different flavour elements it contains. Serving temperature is quite literally a matter of taste!

As more bars need increasing amounts of refrigeration and cold-room equipment to cater for a greater variety of beers, the serving temperature of stout, particularly draught stout, can fluctuate erratically. For

The strength of Guinness varies worldwide. In Ireland and England it's 4% ABV. In the U.S.A., it's over 5%. In Continental Europe, it ranges from 6-8%, while in Africa, Australia and Asia, it's as high as 8%.

example, while the average summer temperature of draught stout poured from Dublin taps is around an acceptable 11°C, some well-known pubs reach a high of over 15°C and others go as low as 5°C. Recently, a Sunday Times travel correspondent experienced complaints in one Dublin pub regarding the cooling of stout 'below lounge temperature - a new practise that was... tantamount to heresy'.

The absolute contempt which American and Australian drinkers reserve for warm beer has become something of a national characteristic and is being exported along with their beers. (In Ireland, Budweiser is served at 4°C, three to five degrees lower than other beers distributed by Guinness).

But wine lovers would be equally

Above: Dublin pub characters by Harry Kernoff, R.H.A.

disgusted with red wine served at less than room temperature. And perhaps the time has come to regard stout as, in some

GUINNESS SPY

During the nineteenth century, a certain Mr. Shand travelled the world as a roving Guinness pub-spy, ensuring that the company standards were being upheld in foreign parts. His hand-written reports are still filed in the deepest recesses of St. James's Gate. And never did his employers have any reason to suspect that his interest in the black stuff was anything other than business-like ■

respects, as closely allied to red wine as it is to your typical colonial thirst-quenchers. For if your favourite tipple has more effect on your teeth than on your taste-buds it's time to ask why.

Despite its name, stout is no more fattening than other beers.

THE BOTTLE

If you're in Limerick, ask for a Danno. In London it's better known as a Rupert. In more prosaic parts, it's simply called the Large Bottle. This range of affectionate pet-names is a measure of the special esteem which discerning stout drinkers all over the world have reserved for the pint bottle of Guinness Extra Stout, for more than a century.

Today, it is something of an endangered species, the only widely available bottle-conditioned stout. Unlike the keg or draught stout, it continues to ferment beyond the brewery gate. So, when bottled Guinness is delivered to your local bar it is still alive, its yeasts and sugars producing sufficient carbon dioxide to give that distinctive bubbly head.

To the purists, bottled Guinness is accepted as 'real ale' because, unlike its cousin on tap, it is unpasteurised (draught Guinness is unpasteurised in Ireland) and

The Guinness family, which subscribed to a minority religion, was once accused of mashing Protestant Bibles and prayer books into the brew to force their faith's ingestion by unwitting Catholic consumers in Ireland.

the carbon dioxide which it contains is the product of natural fermentation rather than a nearby cylinder. As no nitrogen has been pumped into it, the gas bubbles which make up the head are less dense and more likely to disappear earlier. You may consider this relative flatness a small price to pay for such a rare taste. But where do you stand on flatulence? Blame it on the natural yeast sediment which you hardly notice at the bottom of a dark brew in a dark bottle.

Ideally, Guinness should be drunk three weeks after bottling, although Guinness says it has an indefinite shelf-life. The company cites the case of Sir Douglas Mawson's 1929 Antarctic expedition. One of the team came across the left-over pro-visions of an expedition made 18 years earlier. These included 'four bottles of Guinness on a shelf, which, although frozen, were put to good use'. No doubt, in more temperate climes, the corks would have popped much earlier.

In Ireland, bottling of Guinness has been centralized at St. James's Gate since the early 1970s. Before then, bottling took place at hundreds of regional premises, a fact proudly displayed on each local label. In Britain, Guinness brewed at the London

Park Royal brewery is transported by tanker for regional bottling.

Oyster Stout, flavoured with real oyster essence enjoyed a brief popularity in the 1930's, notably on the Isle of Man.

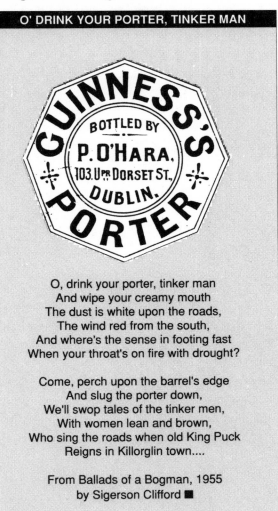

O' DRINK YOUR PORTER, TINKER MAN

O, drink your porter, tinker man
And wipe your creamy mouth
The dust is white upon the roads,
The wind red from the south,
And where's the sense in footing fast
When your throat's on fire with drought?

Come, perch upon the barrel's edge
And slug the porter down,
We'll swop tales of the tinker men,
With women lean and brown,
Who sing the roads when old King Puck
Reigns in Killorglin town....

From Ballads of a Bogman, 1955
by Sigerson Clifford ■

STOUT
REPASTS

For a hangover take the juice of two quarts of whiskey...

Eddie Condon

WITH FOOD

Stout has, over the years, struck up an amiable partnership with various solid forms of nourishment, as either an accompaniment or an ingredient. In the former category, stout and oysters is rightly regarded as one of life's great delicacies. For what it's worth, Benjamin Disraeli is known to have enjoyed this particular combination on the night of November 21 1837, 'the most remarkable day hitherto of my life'. The brewers of Bridgeport stout say that it 'complements spicy foods of all kinds and is ideally suited to oysters and other shellfish'. (Some people object to the allegedly slimy texture of oysters, however).

In Ireland, a more likely accompaniment around that time would have been crubeens or boiled pig's feet, a delicacy which has, for some mysterious reason, suffered a decline in popularity over the past two decades. Perhaps it has something to do with the fact that pigs insist on keeping only a fraction of a smidgen of a percentage of their meat in their trotters, the rest being fat and bone. Or is it that a crubeen must be held while eating, giving your hands the same relationship to superglue as Macbeth's had to blood? Either way, whatever flavour crubeens possess is measurably enhanced by both literal and liquid darkness.

In these more affluent times, Irish diners are just as likely to match meatier parts of the pig (or cow, or lamb) with stout. Stout is most often used in the kitchen as a tasty adjunct to the stock used in beef stews and casseroles. As with coq-au-vin, the beverage has the effect of flavouring and tenderising the meat. It is

scratch

In the jungles of Brazil, the naturalist T.W. Hinchliff found that...' the best remedy that I know for over-exertion in a hot climate consists simply of drinking a bottle of Guinness before doing anything else. The cure is instantaneous'.

also an indispensable ingredient of porter cake, Christmas pudding and Christmas cake. Apart from its distinctive burnt malty flavour, it adds some necessary darkness to the final colour. Matilda Bay Brewing Company in Fremantle recommends that you accompany its Brass Monkey Stout with oysters, Moet or Stilton cheese.

The brewers of Newquay Stout claim that their product is 'especially good with cream based pies, soups and pasta dishes - a real treat at Christmas with rich sweet pies and puddings".

Some cooks recommend the addition of a half pint of stout to your favourite canned soup. Others have very definite views on the type of stout used, preferring the less bitter brews. The sweeter stouts have sometimes been used even to make desserts.

So, even if it's peanuts or crisps, fish and chips or burgers, Chinese take-away or pizza, stout has the taste to go with them.

WITH OTHER DRINKS

While for the afficionado, the idea of mixing the beloved Black Stuff with another drink is anathema, this dubious practice does exist, resulting in some names as bizarre as the mixture itself:

Black Velvet: Half fill a glass with stout and top up with champagne or sparkling wine. Or tonic water, or champagne cider, or mineral water. Reputedly invented in 1861 by the barman at Brook's Club in St. James's, London to commemorate the death of Albert, who ran a well-known museum with his wife Victoria. The following year, when Bismarck visited England, he probably tasted it; for a long time afterwards it was known as a 'Bismark'. A variation on this is a half part stout, quarter part champagne and quarter part vodka, christened 'Rocket Fuel' for obvious reasons.

Black and Tan: A mixture of equal parts stout and ale popular in the UK where its title does not have the historical connotations still lingering in Ireland. In Australia, a mixture of Cooper's Extra Stout and Cooper's Sparkling Ale has found favour amongst devotees of bottle-conditioned beer. US President George Bush is on record as having quaffed two pints of Black and Tan back in 1985, when he was Vice-President.

Stout Shandy: Officially consists of equal parts stout and lemonade, which some unscrupulous barmen interpret as meaning a glassful of lemonade and a dollop of stout. A grand thirst-quencher as long as you don't overdo the sweet stuff. Known in New Zealand as an All Black Shandy and in Australia as Portergaff, a mixture of Porter and Shandygaff. Incidentally, Shandygaff, a mixture of beer and gingerbeer, was reputedly Ray Milland's favourite drink while filming The Lost Weekend.

A bottled Guinness Shandy is available in certain countries, while a non-alcoholic Guinness Malta is on sale in more tropical climes.

Wasp Sting: is a variation of the above, replacing lemonade with orange juice.

Liverpool Kiss: Take a sip off the top of your glass and replace it with a shot of Blackcurrant Cordial.

Stout Cooler: Cover the bottom of your glass with 1/6 measure of Dubonnet, 1/3 liqueur glass of Curacao, 1/3 liqueur glass of Creme de Cacao (ice cube optional). Fill with stout.

Snake Bite: One-third stout and two-thirds cider.

STIN

By Myles na gCopaleen

In this brief discourse I intend to be, after, my fashion, serious; and I expect attention. Now *(turns to scrub blackboard, suddenly clasps hand to back of neck and wheels around scarlet)*: Stand up the boy with the catapult!

(Silence)

If that happens again there will be wholesale finings. Now consider this word here:

ZYTHOS.

That means a fermented drink made from barley. Make a note of it. It is the Greek for Guinness. The Latin is, of course, this

CERVISIA

It is from that you get the Spanish for Guinness - cerveza. I hope that all that is clear. Cervisia sounds like what a villainous Continental waiter mutters every time he serves you with a Guinness. He is looking for money so pay no attention.

There is a notion - but current only in Ireland - that the wittiest people in the world are the Irish. Wrong, of course. The wittiest are the French. Only the French could devise the word they have for "stout", They call it porter!

Here, now is perhaps the most important word of all:

Continued on Page49

Porter by Jack B Yeats.

Sam Weller composing his Valentine. A drawing by H.K. Browne from the Pickwick Papers by Charles Dickens.

Tumbril: A mixture of stout, port, brandy (and champagne if available) available only on prescription from your family doctor. Also known as 'La Guillotine' the last resort of unfortunate souls who are 'dying' from a hangover.

Chaser: Popular with the older Irish stout drinker, this involves sipping 'a drop' of Irish whiskey before, after or between drinks of stout. Punters have also been known to add the whiskey to the pint.

Sheffield Stout: Is a non-alcoholic regional variation consisting of Mather's Black Beer and lemonade.

Dublin Depth Charge: Replace the top half-inch of your pint with a shot of rum.

Half and Half: An American version of

BARLEY

Barley is nothing more, believe me, than a form of grass. Latin *gramen*. I remember when I was a young chap at College, a friend complained bitterly to me that his girlfriend had repeatedly been late keeping dates, and he put this unpunctuality down to secret stoutbibbing. I almost forgot to mention by the way, that the Greek for yeast is

ZELOS

and I regret to say that this word otherwise means passion, ardour, desire. However, I consider myself a poet of sorts - you have, of course, read "Leaves of Grass" by Malt Whitman? - and I reproved my young friend in the following lines:

> *Appointments not kept*
> *Tempt some men to say*
> *That ladies should rigidly*
> *Stick to their tay.*
> *It's alleged they delayed*
> *Before they came out*
> *Inside in the kitchen*
> *To scoff a large stout -*
> *Varium et mutabile femina*
> *Cannot fairly be blamed on the grame-*
> *na.*

He did not like it. I need hardly tell you, nor a subsequent joke about "grass widows". But that, I think, is all I have to say.

Heavens, I nearly forgot! That word Stin in my title may puzzle some people. Divil a mystery about it all. Stin is something many good people are partial to during Lent.

STIN is the opposite of STOUT ■

Black and Tan, which involves topping up your favourite beer with an equal amount of stout.
Stout Sangaree: Warmed stout topped with nutmeg.

You may also hear of stout being mixed with port, lime, tomato juice, milk, cider, advokaat, your own homebrew and almost anything else on the shelf. Whatever you're having yourself...

MESSAGE
IN A
BOTTLE

... the foaming ebon ale which the noble twin brothers... those cunning brothers, lords of the vat...

James Joyce

There are over 10,000 pubs in Ireland dispensing 200,000 pints of Guinness a day.

I n 1954, one of the most eccentric of Guinness publicity stunts involved 150,000 bottles floating in the world's major ocean. Inside, the prospective finder was invited to reply to Guinness. Those who did included a Mexican prisoner and an Eskimo boy. A similar exercise today would no doubt cause outrage and controversy on the grounds of marine pollution.

Stout advertising has always been colourful. The advertising agencies had an obvious dilemma: whether to represent the typical stout drinker as white-collared, blue-collared or agricultural. They got around the problem by using fantasy, and created an entire menagerie of colourful beasts combined with memorable humans.

THE GREAT SANDOW

Strongmen have been used to advertise stout since the beginning of the century. An early example of what we would now call 'character merchandising' appears on a Murphy label dated December 1892. Underneath a picture of a circus strongman lifting a horse, an endorsement reads: 'Dear Sir, From experience I can strongly recommend Messers JJ Murphy's stout'. It is signed; 'Eugene Sandow'.

Sandow was born in Eastern Europe in 1867. The 1891 World Weightlifting Champion toured the British Isles as a sort of human forklift, raising above his head horses, pianos and anything guaranteed to

**Sandow goes
through his paces.**

MURPHYS Stout

GIVES STRENGTH

wring a gasp from his astonished audience.

This strongman motif was used by Murphy in stylised form on its labels until the 1960s. However, to this day a similar strongman appears on the label of a stout brewed by McCallum Breweries in Sri Lanka. It is called Sando Stout. So, did Sando's act travel as far as Ceylon? And was his audience as impressed as the audience in the Palace Theatre, Cork? Or did he simply have an enterprising manager to exploit to the maximum the commercial potential which he knew his client possessed?

Ironically, Sandow died in 1925 after lifting a car out of a ditch. However, he has the unique distinction of having been commemorated by two different brands of stout, each brewed on opposite sides of the world. In the early 1930s, Guinness used a fictional character called Henry Hercules who performed such incredible feats as lifting cars and pianos - with a little help from the black stuff of course.

It's now over ten years since the demise of that multi-million pound disaster known as Guinness Light. And they said it couldn't be done!

THE TOUCAN

Bring us back a parrot, mister'. This was the taunt hurled at Guinness bargemen as they ferried wooden barrels of stout the short distance from St. James's Brewery to waiting ships in Dublin Port. However, if the Guinness bargemen failed to return with an exotic bird, the Guinness agencies did not.

In 1935, the graphic artist most closely associated with the classic Guinness ads, John Gilroy, was scouting around for new recruits for his menagerie of furred and feathered stout-drinkers. He saw potential

TOCO-TOUCANS
Presented to the Zoo by
Messrs. Arthur Guinness Son & Co. Ltd., 1950

**Below: A Guinness
poster with John
Gilroy's friends.**

in the rhyme about the pelican whose 'bill can hold more than his belly can'. It would be another four years before his pelican appeared holding 'in its beak enough for a week'. However, it was not accompanied by the text, the final line 'I simply don't know how the hell he can' probably being considered too crude.

Instead, the famous detective-story writer, Dorothy L Sayers, nipped a few feathers here, tucked a little beak there and cut the bird's consumption by over two-thirds with... 'just think what Toucan do'. For the next quarter-century, the toucan and his friends would represent the typical Guinness-drinker.

Although killed off by official decree in 1961, the toucan, like his cousin the

phoenix, arose from the ashes in 1979. Talking this time, he survived until 1982, when a new sheriff with new ideas arrived in town.

His name was Ernest Saunders.

One cannot laugh.

But Toucan.

MY GOODNESS!

Today, the idea that an alcoholic drink could double as a form of medicine is a curious one. Yet, that very idea has been the cornerstone of one of the most successful advertising campaigns of this century.

When the slogan 'Guinness is Good For You' first appeared in 1928, it was not a particularly original idea, but merely reinforced what stout-drinkers already wanted to believe. The combination of a dark, opaque colour, a contrasting white head and bitter taste had already singled it out as an ideal folk medicine. It provided a perfect foil to the pro-temperance, anti-pleasure lobby. It was the perfect rationalisation: 'Don't think for a moment that I'm actually ENJOYING this black, bitter stuff - I'm just drinking it as a tonic!' And so into popular folklore and

Many people mistakenly believe that stout is 'full of iron', making it 'good for you'. In fact, most beers have about the same iron content.

In 1815, one of Wellington's officers, wounded in the Battle of Waterloo, wrote..."I felt the most extra-ordinary desire for a glass of Guinness... and I am confident that it contibuted more than anything else to my recovery".

mythology went such characters as The Man Who On His Death-bed Refused To Drink The Glass Of Guinness Offered By The Doctor.

For Guinness, it was a question of pushing an open door: 'It is doubtful whether, at the outset, there was much thought given to the truth of this statement..., it was enough that people either already believed it to be true, or were prepared to believe it'. (1)

Of course, Guinness, never a slouch when it came to self-promotion, was not slow to capitalise on this happy set of circumstances. In an age less sophisticated than our own, the medical profession was coaxed, with a combination of flattery and free samples into providing testimonials for use in advertising. Throughout the 1930s, 1940s and 1950s, Guinness produced two dozen annual booklets of whimsical verse and colour illustration specifically for distribution to doctors at Christmas time.

And the testimonials arrived, testifying to the miraculous benefits of the stuff for all kinds of ailments - anaemia, insomnia, neuralgia, depression, constipation and under-nourished brain cells. It gave strength, calmed 'nerves', aided digestion, cured exhaustion, improved blood, increased virility. All in marked contrast to the present-day pronouncements of the medical profession on the subject of alcoholic beverages.

In Britain, nursing mothers could qualify for stout on the National Health Scheme, while in Ireland miniature bottles of Guinness, known as Snipes, were provided to convalescents up to the 1970s.

In what are now commonly referred to as

Draught Guinness is four times more popular than its bottled cousin.

One of the famous Guinness posters depicting superhuman strength achieved by the drinking of Guinness.

Unpasteurised stout is an excellent source of Folic Acid, which is of particular benefit to women who are pregnant or breast-feeding.

developing countries, this phenomenon took the form of an emphasis on the aphrodisiac and virility-enhancing qualities of the potion. It became common in Asiatic countries to bathe new-born babies in stout.

So, 'in the cold,grey light of dawn' (as ad persons might say), when stripped of the myths and half-truths, what is the connection between stout and nutrition?

BARLORE

On arrival at your local bar from the brewery, the typical stainless steel keg holds about 90 pints of beer. At this stage, it has a maximum shelf-life of three months. After delivery, kegs may be stored in a temperature-controlled Cold Room. In Summer, three days are needed to bring the temperature down from 80°C to an average 8° - 10°C. In Winter, two days are sufficient for a drop in temperature from around 60°C. At its simplest, your beer may come from a keg underneath the counter, through a cooler which is also located under the counter. A more sophisticated cooling system involves enclosing the beer lines in refrigerated casing from cold room to tap. The gas cylinder used to pump stout contains a mixture of approximately 30% Carbon Dioxide and 70% Nitrogen ■

Essentially, stout is a pleasant drink and very little else. As with most beers, its food and nutritional value is minimal in the context of a normal daily diet.

It contains approx 200 kilocalories of energy per pint as well as alcohol. The protein, sugars, sodium, potassium, calcium, iron, copper, riboflavin, niacin, pyridoxine, pantothenic acid, vitamin B12, and biotin which it also contains are represented in more substantial quantities in a normal, everyday diet. Because many of these nutrients are contained in the yeast, pasteurisation kills much of the food value of stout.

Perhaps an argument could be made that at the beginning of the century the average stout-drinker did not have access to such a wide variety of nutritional sources. Maybe a convalescent who is incapable of taking solid food will benefit from drinking stout. It is possible that the psychosomatic value of stout as a tonic has had beneficial effects. But these are flimsy threads on which to hang an argument for what is in essence, a uniquely tasteful drink. That alone is reason enough to drink it.

Stout dispenser in a state of undress...

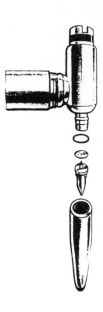

(1) Brian Sibley: 'Guinness Advertising' (Guinness Superlatives, 1985).

Recent Guinness advertisement

STOUTS
ABROAD

I shall put myself outside a pint of Guinness.

Robert Louis Stevenson

In 1980 the average Irish consumption of beer was 214 pints per head. By 1988 however, this figure was down to 116.

One popular Irish comedian defines his fellow countryman as 'a complex mechanism for turning Guinness into urine'.

Although, contrary to the national stereotype, the Irish drinker is at the bottom of the Top Twenty Beer-Drinking nations, almost half the beer consumed in Ireland is stout. Of every ten pints of stout bought, nine are likely to be Guinness, with Murphy's slightly ahead of Beamish on the remainder. Not surprisingly, Ireland is also Europe's leading stout exporting country. While the majority of this is Guinness, Murphys sell more stout in Britain than in Ireland.

Irish people tend to regard stout as an Irish phenomenon, but a great variety of stouts is brewed in the most unlikely and far flung parts of the globe. In Europe stout production is largely confined to Ireland, England and Scandinavia. Draught Guinness Export, brewed in Dublin to the standards of the German Purity Law, is available on a limited scale in Germany. Bottled Guinness Foreign Extra can be bought in supermarkets and other outlets throughout Continental Europe. You are also likely to find this brew in Africa, the

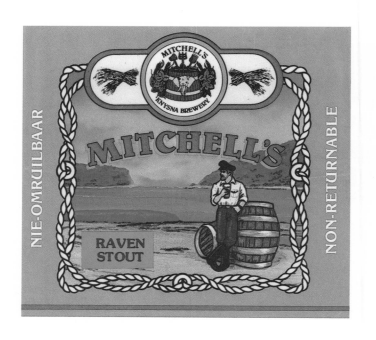

NIE-OMRUILBAAR

NON-RETURNABLE

MITCHELL'S

RAVEN STOUT

CASTLEMAINE PERKINS LTD. 11 FINCHLEY STREET, MILTON, QUEENSLAND

CARBINE STOUT

750 ML

5.1% ALC/VOL

PRODUCT OF AUSTRALIA

SOVEREIGN BREWERY

OLD GOLD STOUT

PURE MALT

375ml   4.9% alc

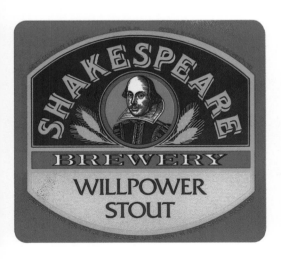

SHAKESPEARE

BREWERY

WILLPOWER STOUT

HOP BACK BREWERY

ENTIRE STOUT

THE HOP BACK BREWERY THE WYNDHAM ARMS, SALISBURY

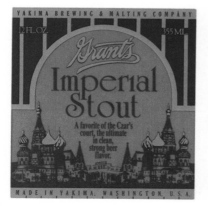

EAGLE HAWK HILL BREWING CO.

BARLEY
STOUT

15¢ Deposit Refund at point of sale S.A.
A PRODUCT OF AUSTRALIA, BREWED AND BOTTLED BY
EAGLE HAWK HILL BREWING CO. SUTTON NSW

330ml ALCOHOL VOL. 7.9%

STRZELECKI BREWERY

MADE IN AUSTRALIA

330 ml 6% Alc Vol

Brewed & Bottled by
STRZELECKI BREWING COMPANY PTY. LTD.
Baromi Road, Mirboo North, Victoria

POWERHOUSE STOUT

CASH BACK BOTTLE

CASCADE

375mL

BREWED AND BOTTLED BY TASMANIAN BREWERIES

156 COLLINS STREET, HOBART. AUSTRALIA 7000

EXPORT STOUT

5.8% ALC/VOL

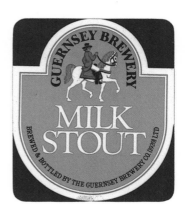

GUERNSEY BREWERY

MILK
STOUT

BREWED & BOTTLED BY THE GUERNSEY BREWERY CO. (029N) LTD

Purest
Ingredients

Finest
Quality

SIERRA NEVADA®
STOUT

This Stout is entirely handmade, in the "old world" tradition, using
only the finest barley malts, whole hops, brewers yeast and water.
BREWED AND BOTTLED BY SIERRA NEVADA BREWING CO., CHICO, CALIF.
NET CONTENTS 12 FL. OZ.

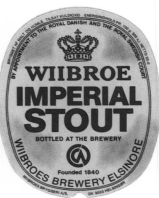

BY APPOINTMENT TO THE ROYAL DANISH AND THE ROYAL SWEDISH COURT

WIIBROE
IMPERIAL
STOUT

BOTTLED AT THE BREWERY

Founded 1840

WIIBROES BREWERY ELSINORE

WIIBROES BRYGGERI A/S.   DK 3000 HELSINGØR

INHOUD 50 CL © EXTRA ZWAAR BIER

TRADE MARK

VAN
VOLLENHOVEN'S
STOUT

STATIEGELD 10 CENT

6.5% VOL. ALC. ANNO 1733 AMSTERDAM

0156

BRIJ VAN DEN BOSSCHE
9560 ST.-LIEVENS-ESSE

Buffalo

Kat. 1 Luxe   e 25 cl. bier.

SWAN STOUT

Swan Stout is brewed in the wood and fermented in the bottle. The finest quality barley malt is blended with roasted malt and hops to ensure an exceptional stout of rich, full bodied flavour.

Brewed and bottled by Cooper & Sons Ltd. under licence for The Swan Brewery Company Limited, Perth, Western Australia.

750ml 6.8% ALC./VOL.

JAMES J MURPHY & COMPANY LIMITED

MURPHY

Extra Stout

BREWED AT LADY'S WELL BREWERY CORK

7% ALC./VOL. 330 ml e

BIRRA DOPPIO MALTO BIÉRE BIER CERVEZA

1886 AWARDED GOLD MEDAL

Samuel Smith's

CONTRACTORS TO HER MAJESTY'S FORCES

AWARDED PRIZE AND SILVER MEDAL BOTTLED BEER 1950

THE OLD BREWERY
Samuel Smith
1758
TADCASTER

IMPERIAL STOUT

PRODUCT OF ENGLAND

JAN FEB MAR APR MAY JUN JLY AUG SEP OCT NOV DEC 89 90 91

BEST BEFORE END

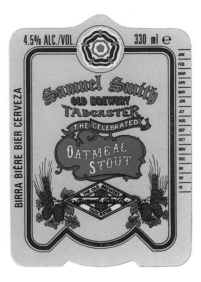

4.5% ALC./VOL. 330 ml e

BIRRA BIÉRE BIER CERVEZA

Samuel Smith
OLD BREWERY
TADCASTER

THE CELEBRATED

OATMEAL STOUT

THE OLD BREWERY
Samuel Smith
TADCASTER

PRODUCT OF ENGLAND

JAN FEB MAR APR MAY JUN JLY AUG SEP OCT NOV DEC 89 90 91

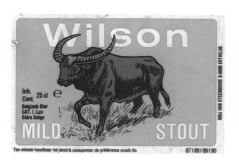

Inh. 25 cl ℮
Cont.
Belgisch Bier
CAT. 1. Lux
Bière Belge

MILD STOUT

BRIJ VAN STEENBERGE B-9000 ERTVELDE

Ten minste houdbaar tot eind/à consommer de préférence avant fin 871881891 90

HOME STOUT

275 ml

BREWED AND BOTTLED BY HOME BREWERY PLC DAYBROOK, NOTTS, ENGLAND

Alc. 3.6% Vol.

Hollandser dan U denkt.

HOME STOUT

TRADE MARK

REGISTERED

BREWED AND BOTTLED BY HOME BREWERY PLC. DAYBROOK, NOTTS. ENGLAND

ORIGINAL GRAVITY 1035°/1039°

275 ml 9.68 fl oz

BEST BEFORE END

Caribbean and Asia. In fact, three million
bottles of Guinness Foreign Extra are sold
daily worldwide.

Yet, scattered here and there, are local
heroes producing stout as part of a range of

A PINT OF PLAIN IS YOU ONLY MAN

When things go wrong and will not come right,
Though you do the best you can
When life looks black as the hour of night -
A pint of plain is your only man.

When money's tight and is hard to get
And your horse has also ran,
When all you have is a heap of debt -
A pint of plain is your only man.

When health is bad and your heart feels strange,
And your face is pale and wan,
When doctors say that you need a change -
A pint of plain is your only man.

When food is scarce and your larder bare
And no rashers grease your pan,
When hunger grows as your meals are rare -
A pint of plain is your only man.

In time of trouble and lousy strife,
You have still got a darling plan,
You can still turn to a brighter life -
A pint of plain is your only man.

By Flann O'Brien
At Swim Two Birds, 1939

If you are in Scotland, watch out for the newest addition to the stout family - Caledonian's Bottled Stout.

beers. In Malta, for instance, Farson's Brewery produces one. There are good reports of stouts made by such independent Canadian breweries as Conners and Spinnakers. In South Africa, Raven Stout has been on sale every winter since 1986, unfiltered, unpasteurised and without preservatives or flavourings. And in Sri Lanka, the Ceylon Brewery produces a prize winning Lion Stout which is fermented in wooden casks.

UNITED KINGDOM

One in every 25 beers drunk in Britain is stout. This comes to over a million barrels of stout a year, and the market is dominated by Guinness. The bottled bottle-conditioned Guinness Extra brewed at Park Royal (as distinct from the pasteurised version in cans and non-returnable bottles) is one of the finest beers available. In Scotland, however, all bottled Guinness is pasteurised.

Tadcaster, in North Yorkshire, is the only town in the world which produces four different types of stout. Three of these are brewed by Samuel Smith, using methods which have changed little over the past two and a half centuries. Water is drawn from

the original wells, 85 feet underneath the brewery, and fermented with a strain of yeast which has been used since the beginning of the century. This fermentation takes place in solid blocks of slate known as Yorkshire Squares which are unique to this brewery. Another unique aspect is the

Above: Guinness poster aimed at the export market.

Some Scandinavian stouts are so strong that at one time they were available only on doctor's prescription.

cooperage, which produces oak barrels for naturally contained cask beers.

Murphy Stout, produced under licence at the Whitbread plant at Magor, South Wales is available in thousands of pubs throughout Britain. Beamish is distributed on draught in cans by Courage. Whitbread produce Britain's most famous indigenous sweet stout, Mackeson. This sweetness results from the inclusion of lactose, a non-fermenting milk sugar. Other varieties of sweet stout include Home Stout, from Nottingham and milk stout from Guernsey in the Channel Islands. Newquay stout is brewed naturally in Redruth, Cornwall, without preservatives in accordance with German purity laws. A cross between a dry and sweet stout, tending more towards the dry, it is available from various supermarket companies such as Tesco, Safeway, Gateway and Waitrose.

SMALL BREWERIES

The brewing of stout has been given a new lease of life within the past twenty years by the growth, chiefly in the UK, US, and Australia of small independent breweries producing a variety of 'handmade' beers.

Many breweries have special arrangements for visitors.

(1) GUINNESS, St. James's Gate, Dublin (ph.: 536700): As an alternative to visiting the actual brewery, the converted Guinness Hop Store hosts a permanent exhibition of the brewing process, past and present. This leads, via an audio-visual presentation and museum, to the tasting bar and the gift shop. Open weekdays 10.00am- 3.00pm.

(2) SAMUEL SMITH, Tadcaster, England (ph.: 32225): Guided tours are available on most working days and evenings. Prior arrangements should be made in writing to the Brewery Visits Organiser.

(3) BRAUHAUS NUSSDORF, Austria: Daily, by reservation.

(4) WIIBROES Brewery, Elsimore, Denmark (ph.: 452 22 1500): Receives 12,000 visitors every year.

(5) YAKIMA Brewing and Malting Co., USA (ph.: 509 575 1900): By appointment only.

(6) MENDOCINO Brewing Co., Hopland, California (ph.: 707 744 1015): Tours by appointment.

Continued on page 71

In 1983, while travelling through the jungles of Borneo, the writer and naturalist Redmond O'Hanlon came across a blanket 'patterned with stylised frogs, deer and crocodiles; and beneath...were woven four glasses, full of Guinness stout'.

What may seem revolutionary is, in fact, merely a return to the norm which existed prior to the monopolisation of the brewing business by multinational companies. It is also the embodiment of a belief that much mass-produced beer has lost some essential qualities. Like taste, for example.

It's all rather like deciding that you've had enough of that soggy white bread you've been eating for years, baked 50 miles away by a company whose ambition is to make water stand up and whose main priority is to ensure that the product have as long a shelf-life as possible. Somewhere along the line essential taste has lost out to commercial expediency. So you decide to bake your own bread, using the best ingredients possible. The end result certainly tastes better. Your friends agree, so you bake a batch for them, too. Soon you're baking on a small scale for a select group of customers who appreciate the difference.

Like baking, brewing on a smaller scale offers a number of advantages. The finest ingredients can be used, and maintenance of the finished product is facilitated. But, crucially, batches may be produced at intervals which do not require the extension of shelf-life by pasteurisation or the removal

(7) SIERRA NEVADA Brewing Co., Chico, California (ph.: 916 893 3520): Tuesday - Sunday, 11.00am - 12.00pm.

(8) BRIDGEPORT Brewing Co., Portland, Oregon (ph.: 503 241 7179): Saturday and Sunday, 2.00pm and 3.00pm.

(9) COOPER'S Brewery, South Australia (ph.: 08 332 5088). Telephone in advance to arrange visits, tours and tasting. The brewery, at 9 Statenborough St., Leadbrook, is five minutes drive from Central Adelaide.

(10) CASTLEMAINE PERKINS, Brisbane (ph.: 07 369 3188). Three tours per day, Monday to Thursday. Book in advance.

(11) MATILDA BAY Brewing Co., North Freemantle, Perth (ph.: 09 430 6222). Telephone the Promotions Representative.

(12) EAGLE HAWK HILL Brewery, Canberra (ph.: 062 416033): Tours during working hours or by appointment.

(13) THE LOADED DOG PUB BREWERY, Melbourne (ph.: 489 8222): Brewery visits arranged by visiting or phoning.

(14) CASCADE Brewery, Hobart, Tasmania: Ring (002) 309111.

(15) SHAKESPEARE Tavern, Auckland, New Zealand: Telephone (09) 735-396.

(16) THE CEYLON Brewery, Numara Eliya, Sri Lanka (ph.: 052-2336): Visits are possible on working days, but a group of more than six is not allowed, on the advice of the Security Forces!

(17) THE GUERNSEY Brewery: Summer season daily Mon. - Fri. 10.30am - 2.30pm (ph.: 0481 720143) ■

of dead yeast by filtration.

While the stout-lover is to some extent aloof from this controversy which revolves largely around lagers and ales, many independent brewers like to produce as many styles of beer as possible, offering the stout drinker an alternative. It also represents a response to the growing niche which has developed in the market in recent years for 'premium' beers.

"BREWER OF THE RAREST STOUT IN BRITAIN"

This is a title which Stephen Simpson-Wells is doing his best to relinquish. For despite nationwide rave reviews his O'Hooligan's Revolt has been available only to residents of his mother's hotel in Penarth, South Wales. However, he is now expanding his brewing operation in an old Elizabethan farmhouse which will supply bottle-conditioned beer for his new pub.

His unique hybrid brewing process involves the use of both malt extract and malted barley in a combination which is economical without compromising on quality. This quality results from a careful balancing of the recipe, in particular the roasted malt. "The quality of the grain is crucial", he says. "With stout, the latitude for error is tighter. You need to be very, very diligent". Once brewed, he likes to mature his beer for up to six months, after which it will hold for a year.

As with others who are passionate on the subject, he has no doubt that the pasteurising and filtering process practised by many commercial brewers effectively kills the essential qualities of the beer. A

If you are worried by the prospect of having to order a demi-litre of stout in a unified Europe, you may be consoled to hear that a spokesman for the E.C. was quoted recently as saying that 'we are not seeking to ride roughshod over national traditions like the Pint. We understand people's sensitivity'.

comparison of Dublin-brewed Guinness with that brewed, for example, in Park Royal, London, reveals the difference in texture and taste which is imparted by the presence of live yeast and dextrins undamaged by pasteurisation.

Stephen Simpson-Wells epitomises in many ways the spirit of independent brewers not only in Britain but world-wide, who believe that it's time to return to brewing as a localised activity providing a distinctive alternative to the bland mass-produced beers of most major breweries. He sees two main problems. "Firstly, brewing is a technical minefield... And secondly, you've got to have an outlet". When the majority of pubs are 'tied' to one or other of the Big Brewers, survival has become an uphill struggle for many independent brewers. But Stephen is confident. "I'm going for a different niche - live draught stout!"

In Britain, CAMRA, the Campaign for Real Ale, has spearheaded opposition to the monopoly which a handful of the major commercial breweries hold on the production and distribution of most British beer. It's annual 'Good Beer Guide' is the best guide to the fluctuating fortunes of Britain's few hundred independent breweries and home-brew pubs regional specialities. While the casualties from year indicate the precarious state of this David and Goliath situation, the general thrust can only bode well for the discerning drinker.

In 1759, Arthur Guinness signed a 9,000 year lease for St. James Gate Brewery at an annual rent of £45.

LONDON SPECIALIST BEER SHOPS

The Bitter Experience, 129 Lee Road, Black Heath SE3 (081-852-8819)
The Beer Shop, 8 Pitfield Street, near Old Street (071-739-3701)
The Grog Blossom, 66 Notting Hill Gate (071-792-3834) or
253 West End Lane, West Hampstead (071-744-7808) or
160 High Road, East Finchley (081-883-3588)

Also, you'll find a full range of Samuel Smith stouts, Courage Imperial stout and others at: The York Beer Shop, 28 Sandringham Street, Fishergate, York (0904 -647136) ■

THE RUSSIAN CONNECTION

Widely-travelled, with impeccable taste and a strength that you will underestimate at your peril, Imperial Russian Stout is the aristocrat of stouts. It has an impressive lineage, royal connections, a colourful history and no little rarity value. It traces its name and origins back to the porters and stouts exported over two centuries ago from England to Russia, where it came under the patronage of Catherine the Great. Shipped to the Baltic in 54-gallon casks called hogsheads, in which it gradually matured while at sea, its characteristic strength and hoppiness

Dutch stouts to watch out for include Arsener, Buffalo and Van Vollenhovens.

helped it survive the long journey to the more northerly parts of Europe where it is still brewed.

Today, the direct descendant of the family is the Imperial Russian Stout brewed by Courage and available from their pubs in selected parts of London and South-East England. Traditionally brewed, it is unpasteurised and matured for two months before continuing to improve in the bottle. It has a shelf-life of five years and at 10% ABV is one of the strongest stouts you are likely to taste.

Samuel Smith's Imperial Stout, brewed in Tadcaster, has a strength of 7%, is unpasteurised and available mainly in the USA. Also available stateside in Boston, San Francisco, Seattle and Portland is Grant's Imperial Stout.

Scandinavian countries have retained the name 'porter' for what is regarded as a prestige product. Carlsberg's brewmaster is adamant that the company's Gammel Carlsberg Porter - Imperial Stout be described as a porter rather than a stout. The Nordic branch of the family have obviously retained the old ancestral title. Gammel is one of the few stouts (sorry! - Porters) to be brewed by bottom

The American marathon runner Frank Shorter was fond of drinking stout the day before a big race in order to build up energy.

fermentation, i.e. using a yeast which ferments at the bottom of the vessel rather than at the top. The Carlsberg subsidiary, Wiibroe, brews a similar product for the Danish market at its brewery in Elsinore. Also in Denmark, the **Ceres** brewery produces a fine stout, while **Albani** prefers to call its version a porter.

DOWN UNDER

Not surprisingly, in the Land of the Amber Nectar stout is a minority taste. Even dropping the serving temperature of Guinness to almost zero hasn't changed the fact that Australian gentlemen prefer blondes. Most of their stout drinking is done in the cooler months, as an alternative to those ubiquitous freezing lagers.

Apart from its coldness, Australian Guinness is almost twice the strength of its Irish counterpart. And that other great example of an Irish dry stout, Murphy's is also available. But these imports have an indigenous rival in the form of the nationally-available Cooper's stout. Naturally-conditioned, unpasteurised and unfiltered, it's well worth a try. Another stout brewed in Adelaide is Old Southwark, overall winner in the 1988 National Beer & Brewing Exhibition. The previous year's winner was Old Gold Stout, brewed by the Sovereign Brewery in Ballarat, one of the 30 or so small breweries in Fremantle. Mean-while, in nearby Perth, Swan stout is brewed under licence by Coopers.

In Melbourne, The Loaded Dog pub brewery offer a **Black Stump** stout. The nearby Stzelecki Brewing Company, which

In 1984, Philip Sexton launched Australia's first micro-brewery, Matilda Bay Brewing Company, producer of Brass Monkey Stout. Today, the company is worth over $23 million.

produced **Powerhouse** stout, has unfortunately, recently gone into receivership.

The **Barley Stout** brewed by the Eagle Hawk Hill Brewing Company in Canberra is closer to a Murphy's than a Guinness.

And just what is it about horses and antipodean stout?

Carbine stout, produced at the Castlemaine Perkins Brewery in Brisbane, takes its name from a famous racehorse. Almost a century later, another Melbourne cup winner, Bonecrusher, is said to have developed a fondness for Guinness!

The dry **Sheaf** stout is an acquired taste from Sydney. In Tasmania, Australia's oldest brewery produces **Cascade** stout. While New Zealanders can enjoy **Willpower** stout at the Shakespeare Tavern in Auckland.

UNITED STATES

Americans call it the Microbrewing Revolution. During the past 20 years, small independent breweries have sprung up throughout the US, producing a range of top-fermenting beers as an alternative to the predominantly bottom-fermented lagers of the giant brewing companies. There are now over 200 microbrewers in the US producing over 1,000 different beers. Some "brewpubs" sell their products in the adjoining bar.

In 1982, California revoked its prohibition laws to allow small breweries to serve their products on the premises. First off the mark was the Mendocino Brewing Company in the appropriately named Hopland, north of San Francisco. Named after a rare local bird, **Black Hawk** stout is made from pale, caramel and black malts, with cluster and cascade hops.

In the north-western city of Yakima, Bert Grant brews a strong **Imperial Stout** from a similar combination of malts, with an infusion of honey. This "thinking man's sipping beer" was voted into first place at the Great American Beer Festival, an award which was later to go to Chico, California, home of **Sierra Nevada Stout**.

The Bridgeport Brewing Company offer **Bridgeport stout** at their adjoining brewpub in Portland, Oregon.

This rare breed of American brewer takes pride in the quality of his product which derives from excellence of ingredients and close attention to all stages of the brewing process.

If you are in New York, try the stout brewed by the Manhattan Brewing Company at 40-42 Thompson Street.

EPILOGUE

*I remember once I drank forty -nine Guinnesses
straight off and I came home on top of a bus.*

Dylan Thomas.

PINT TAKEN

As with all great pleasures, over-indulgence may often result in unwelcome aftereffects. In the case of your favourite tipple, the results are well-enough known. What is less well-known is the difference between fact and fancy when it comes to causes and cure.

For starters, everyone is aware of the direct relationship between **quantity** of alcohol consumed and severity of aftereffects. And, of course, the length of **time** taken to consume this quantity. In other words, if you drink ten pints in two hours, don't expect sympathy next morning from your partner who only drank two pints in ten hours. Hangover effects also vary with sex, mood and body size.

There are other variables which you would do well to bear in mind. There may be no known scientific basis for the old adage that you shouldn't mix your drinks but it is possible that mixing drinks creates new chemical combinations which may cause damage. So don't blend the grape with the grain.

Hangovers vary with drinks. This is because the quantity of congeners differs. Congeners are chemical substances which are present in all drinks to varying degrees. While their exact nature is uncertain, included under the generic term are:

1. Traces of the more dangerous Amyl, Methyl and Butyl alcohols (as distinct from the more familiar Ethyl)

2. Unfermented particles which use your stomach as a fermentation vessel

3. Chemical additives

4. A combination of the above.

Bourbon, for example, contains 95 times more congeners than vodka. Stout and other have a higher congener strength than white wine, gin, vodka, but contain less than any of the darker spirits and wines.

'Line the stomach': there are sound logical reasons for the off-quoted advice to get some soakage in.

Invariably, sound advice is not taken, and occasionally a drinker will awaken 'dying' after a night on the tear. What's to be done?

The first priority is to replace as soon as possible the large quantities of water used by your body to expel alcohol (by sweating and urination). Drink plenty of it before your body starts screaming for water. A glass of cool, carbonated water will never taste better.

There are other things to take. Orange juice will help replace lost vitamin C. For a headache, take Paracetemol rather than Aspirin which will tend to irritate your stomach. If your stomach is upset, take some antacid tablets.

You won't need to be told that you need sleep when every muscle is calling out for it, but do remember to drink as much water as possible beforehand, to avoid waking. Have a glass of water handy in case you do wake: it will maximise your chances of returning to sleep.

Although there are sound medical reasons for drinking tea, coffee or cola, the reality is that you'll drink only what you feel you can stomach. Similarly, an elaborate mythology has built up around hangover cures. But if you can take charcoal tablets, raw fish or raw eggs, there's a good argument that you don't need a cure in the first place. However, it is reported that chemists at Hoffman-La Roche, who gave us Valium, have discovered a substance called R015 - 4513, which has the effect of sobering up its recipient within minutes.

Meanwhile, eat as much of what you can - it will help restore your blood sugar level.

BIBLIOGRAPHY

Michael JACKSON: New World Guide to Beer (Bloomsbury, 1988)
Michael JACKSON: Pocket Beer Book
(Mitchell Beazley, 1986)
Brian SIBLEY: Guinness Advertising (Guinness Superlatives, 1985)
Ted PARRAT: Name Your Poison! (Hale, 1990)
Peter McCALL: The Brewer's Dictionary (Amateur Winemaker, 1986)
Andrea GILLIES (ed.): Good Beer Guide (Camra, 1990)
Jancis ROBINSON: On The Demon Drink (Mitchell Beazley, 1988)
Willie SIMPSON (ed.): Australian Beer Magazine, No. 1.
(Australian Beer Magazine Pty Ltd.)
Willie SIMPSON (ed.): The Australian Beer Guide, No. 2.
(Federal Publishing Co. Pty Ltd.)
Bob PRITCHARD: 'All About Beer' (Amateur Winemaker, 1983)
C.J.J. BERRY: 'Homebrewed Beers and Stouts' (1984)
Andrew O'GORMAN: Bartending for Pleasure and Profit (A. O'Gorman)
An Introduction to Bartending Skills for the Hotel,
Catering and Tourism Industry (CERT, 1987)
Dr. Alan Maryon DAVIS: 'PSSST: A Really Useful Guide to Alcohol'
(Pan, 1989)
David OUTERBRIDGE: 'The Hangover Handbook' (Pan, 1981)
Redmond O'HANLON: 'Into The Heart of Borneo' (Penguin)